Sharks
For Kids

Amazing Animal Books
for Young Readers

By John Davidson

Mendon Cottage Books

JD-Biz Publishing

Download Free Books!
http://MendonCottageBooks.com

Read More Amazing Animal Books

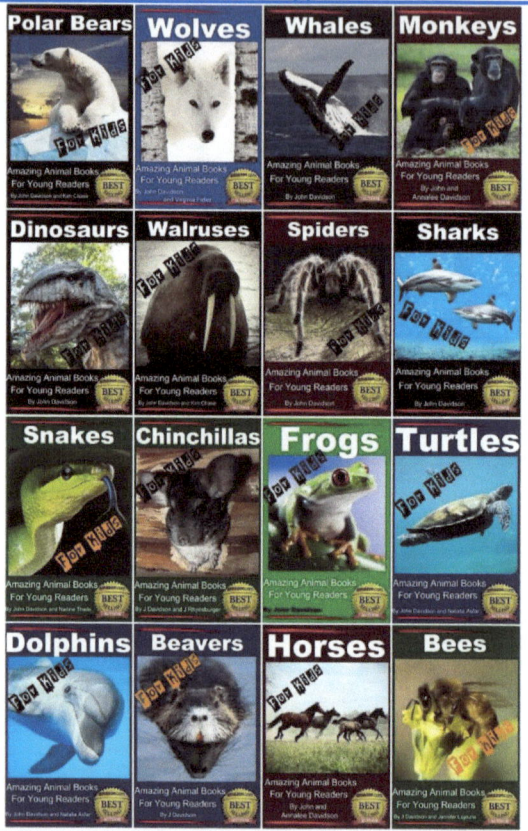

Purchase at Amazon.com

Download Free Books!
http://MendonCottageBooks.com

Table of Contents

1. Introduction to Sharks

Introduction to sharks

Fresh water sharks are known to be of some great interest to the aquarium This is when this fish that appears unusual creates motion in the water through gliding backwards and forwards in its very colorful school. In the introduction to sharks, this article is going to high light some of the commonly found types of sharks, which are best suitable to rear in the aquarium.

Shark catfish with white tip

This type of catfish has a catlike head, with a sleekly body. It is also considered very mellow, as it is known for eating very much. Shark catfish with white tip can survive in brackish, fresh or salty water. In addition to this, this type of fish enjoys associating in groups besides growing too big. This gives the reasons why they should be kept in tanks of larger sizes, and the temperature of such tanks be regulated not to go below 78°F and not to surpass 82°F.

The red tailed shark

This type of sharks prefer either a tube, a cave or a pipe in order to be happy. Red tails grow up to a size of five inches big, and are always kept in schools of not less than six. Sometimes, keeping the alone is not that harmful. These type of fish are always grayish in color with red tails. The recommended water temperature for this fish species should range between 76° to 80°F.

Red Tailed Shark

Rainbow shark

This type of sharks are also kept either singly, or in a group of more than six per aquarium. This is because of their crankiness nature with the others in case they are reared in a low number. Just like the Red tails, rainbow also requires caves, pipes or tubes in order to be happy and active. They are rash berry-orange in color on their tails as well as fins. They are sturdy and aggressive. They grow up to a size of nine inches, and survive in the temperature of about eighty degrees.

Baal shark

This type of shark is even tempered in addition to being hyper. They survive in a water temperature of about 72 to 82 degrees. They are silver in color. Their tails and fins are black tipped and they enjoy associating in larger groups.

2. Great White Shark Facts

Great white sharks normally have 3,000 teeth which are arranged in some rows. The teeth they have in the first row are mainly used for cutting and grabbing the food they eat. The rest of the teeth in the back will replace the ones in front when they fall out are worn down or broken. All the shark's teeth have a triangle shape with jags on their edges. The favorite meal for sharks is fish. They also love eating other animals like sea lions and seals.

Great White Shark © Pieter De Pauw - Fotolia.com

Characteristics

The underside of the great white is colored white and the back is colored gray. These sharks have 3 major fins; two on the side (pectoral) and one on the back (dorsal). All great white sharks have five gill slits. Once it has finished nine years after birth, it becomes an adult. Every year, the shark grows for about 25 to 30 centimeters. Their average length is 4.5 meters when they stop growing. The largest shark can be as long as 6.5 meters.

Where they live

All great white sharks have the sea as their home. They love staying near the coast, especially where there is warm water. Sometimes, they will make dives and swim in the deep waters of the ocean. They can comfortably live in water that is as shallows as 3 feet deep or as deep as 1,300 meters.

Great white sharks and humans

In very rare cases, great white sharks will attack humans. They do not attack humans because they love to eat people. Sharks are very curious. When they see something they do not know they will bite it to find out more about it. For example, when they see a surfboard, they will bite it to find out what it is. In some cases, great white sharks will see the shadows of people surfing and attack them because the shadows look like seals.

3. Bull Shark Facts

Have you ever heard of Bull sharks? Here are important facts that you should know about them.

Bull Shark © Ian Scott - Fotolia.com

1. Bull sharks have a scientific name called Carchahinus leucas.

---

2. They are found in waters such as Atlantic coast in the United States starting from Massachusetts in the north to Mexico.

3. Bull sharks like living in waters that are shallow, you can readily find them in lagoons, river mouths and bays. They sometimes stay in fresh waters especially the fresh water rivers bordering the oceans.

4. Bull sharks take about 6 years to mature; their lifespan is about 14 years.

5. They can reach a length of 11.5 feet when fully mature.

6. Bull sharks are threatened by being over fished as they grow at a slower rate.

7. Bull sharks can be caught by fishermen using different fishing methods such as the line, hooks, gill net and trawling.

8. Bull sharks are well adapted as predators by having strong teeth that are being replaced throughout their lifetime.

9. They are sensitive to smell and have sense receptors that can sense far distances.

10. Their eyes can easily adapt to low light levels in the sea and on the surface of water. This makes them maneuver easily in deep waters in search for food

11. Have lateral line receptors which assist them greatly in sensing any movement made in the water.

12. They have strong electroreceptor that helps them in sensing electrical fields made by their prey distances away.

13 .Bull sharks are the most dangerous among the various sharks in the world; they are highly aggressive and keep hunting in shores of waters.

14 .Bull sharks feed on foods such as birds, bony fish, dolphins, terrestrial mammals, echinoderms and even other small sharks of different species including their own species.

15. The existence of bull sharks is threatened by humans

where they are being killed mainly for their fins which are being used in traditional Chinese dish called shark-fin soup.

.

4. Tiger Shark Facts

Do you know that tiger sharks are the fourth biggest shark in the whole world? They can grow very big and long; an adult tiger shark can reach 20 to 25 feet long. Their weight is even more impressive; they can weigh up to 2,000 pounds. Just imagine one of those in your pool or lake?

Tiger sharks are called tigers because when they are young, they have dark vertical stripes in their body. But when they become adult sharks, the stripes go away. They are mostly found in tropical and warm waters close to the shores, and are considered very dangerous for human and animals. Normally sharks like to attack you and then leave you alone. Tiger sharks are not like that they will attack you, and then stick around to attack you again. Not a very good thing do you think? They are considered man eaters, but luckily these kinds of attacks haven't happened a lot.

With their great sense of sight and sensitive smell receptors they can tell where to go to find their next meal. They can actually sense their next victim from very far away. Their teeth are so sharp and serrated, and their jaw so powerful, that they can even crack a sea turtle shell or a clam shell. Because they have a limitless menu in their diet, they have no problem finding food all year around.

Tiger Shark and Giant Trevelly fish in Maui tropical waters

There are so many other fun facts about tiger sharks, for instance they grow slowly and take many years to mature (normally from 12 to 18 years). This fact makes them vulnerable. Many of them have been hooked by people that are fishing. Another interesting fact is that their eyes adapt very quickly to a low light area.

Tiger Shark © Christopher Bartlett - Fotolia.com

Do you want to learn more about these powerful and

interesting fish? Go to your local library with your parents or search online to learn more about tiger sharks.

5. Hammerhead Shark Facts

Hammerhead sharks get their names from the structure of their head which is flattened and has an extension that looks like a hammer. Their hammered heads have sensors that assist it in finding food in water by receiving electric signals from other living creatures. This helps them locate food and also escape from danger.

Here are some amazing hammerhead shark facts: .

1. There are 9 species of the hammered sharks with each of the species having its own specific characteristics. The biggest of the 9 species is the great hammerhead shark that may weigh up to 500 pounds.

2. The hammerhead sharks do not lay eggs like other fish do. Instead, they give birth to their young ones. The young ones of the sharks are called pups. The females give birth to between 12 to 15 pups. After giving birth the female sharks do not take care of their young ones. Once the pups are born,

they usually swim to warm waters where they stay until they have grown up.

Hammerhead Shark © gabbo - Fotolia.com

3. Hammered sharks have a gray brown upper body color and a white belly. The white belly helps them not to be easily seen by their prey since the surface of the ocean has a color that blends in with their belly color. When in their natural habitats the hammer sharks can live for up to between 20 to 30 years.

4. The eyes of hammered sharks are located the sides of their hammered head. This gives them the ability to see both above and below them at all times. This is an advantage for them when looking for food.

5. They have a small mouth compared to the size of their heads and feed on a variety of smaller organisms such as fish and squids.

6. During the day, hammerhead sharks swim in large groups called schools while at night they usually go hunting alone.

6. Whale Shark Facts

Some whale shark facts are very interesting. This is because most children think a whale shark eats people at the beach. A whale shark is unlikely to attack you when you are out at the sea. This is because a whale shark is a very gentle animal. It can even allow you to swim around it. The only time it will attack you is if you provoke it or try to attack it. This animal is big and long. The whale shark is the world's largest fish. The male whale shark is bigger than the female.

Whale Shark © zeamonkeyimages - Fotolia.com

To see the size of this animal, you can visit a zoo or an organization that keeps whale sharks. When you are in such an organization, ask the people working there about interesting whale shark facts. Usually you will find it hard to see a whale shark in its natural habitat at the ocean. This is because it is always moving from one ocean to the next. We call this movement migration. If you are lucky, you will one day see a whale shark in an ocean. This animal can migrate to different oceans in the world. Migration helps it to look for food and a mate. Its favorite food is fish and different small creatures found in the sea.

Bad people hurt and kill whale sharks. People in some countries hunt the whale sharks for its meat. Others believe that the whale shark's body parts are a form of medicine. Such people are reducing the number of whale sharks and putting this animal in danger. A whale shark can live to 100 years old but some of them are killed before they give birth. To help prevent this, you can ask your parents to assist you to join organizations fighting to protect whale sharks.

7. Shark Attack Facts

Shark Attack © Mike_Kiev - Fotolia.com

Every year there are more than 50 to 70 shark attacks all over the world. The numbers have also increased more than previous years but not due to the reason the sharks are so aggressive. In the U.S state coastal, lightning hits and kills over 41 people every year. National geographic has given news about surprising shark facts. More than 375 shark species have been discovered but only some dozen are regarded as very dangerous. Three species are mainly responsible for human attacks. They are tiger, great white and bull sharks. Sharks kill over 20 people a year they suffer highly at human hands. Over 20 to 100 million sharks are dying every year because of fishing activity based on the data from the natural history's shark attack file. The company also estimates that certain shark populations have raised thirty to fifty percent.

World's speediest shark is the Shortfin Mako and it can speed up to 20 miles an hour. It can possibly swim faster than this speed. They are fast to catch fleetest fish like swordfish and tuna. Whale shark is the largest shark that can grow up to 60 feet length. The big shark eats small plankton. The deep water dogfish shark is the smallest shark species and it has a length of about eight inches. Sharks are called as eating machines. Due to the reason lot of species are cold blooded, certain sharks consume up to two percent of the body weight daily. Scientists are still researching about shark migration. Blue sharks roam on the north Atlantic and it can swim up to 3740 nautical miles to other countries like Brazil. Certain sharks should swim steadily to breathe air from water traveling by their gills. Other sharks can attain this when stationary. They experience substitute periods of activity and rest but do not sleep.

8. Shark Behavior

Though sharks are fish they are different from other kinds of fish in various ways. The skeleton of a shark is made of cartilage while the skeleton of other fish are of bones. Like most other fish sharks breathe through gills, but they have six or seven gill slits on both sides while the other fish have only one gill slit. While most other fish have flap that covers the gill slits sharks do not possess flaps. Sharp tooth-like scales cover the body of shark these scales are called tentacles, but the other fish's body are covered with smooth and flat scales.

Sharks are dangerous. But it cannot be said that they are a threat to human. Actually it is man who poses a threat to sharks. Every year millions of sharks are being killed by fishermen and even many species of sharks are in danger of extinction. There are different kinds of sharks. Angel sharks, saw sharks, dogfish sharks, ground sharks, mackerel sharks, carpet sharks, bull head sharks and frilled and cow sharks are the main types of sharks. Studies prove that the types of sharks living now have evolved even before hundreds million years.

Shark Skeleton © ia_64 - Fotolia.com

A strong power of smelling is a unique feature of sharks. They can even spot their prey from a mile distance away just by smell. They also have an extremely strong hearing capacity. They can hear sounds from a place more than seven hundred feet away. Lower sounds that are not audible to humans are audible to sharks.

Studies have been done on shark behavior. It has been shown that the shark behavior is influenced by different factors like water temperature and the time of the day. Moon also influences the shark behavior. Sharks dive deeper during summer and they remain closer to the surface during winter seasons when the deeper water is colder.

9. Shark Anatomy

When you try to think of what a shark looks like, does anything immediately come to mind? Well of course we know that sharks have a big fin on their back, a long snout like nose and big sharp teeth in their mouths don't they? After all that's what makes them so scary. Can you imagine swimming in the ocean and seeing that silver fin circling around you? Not fun.

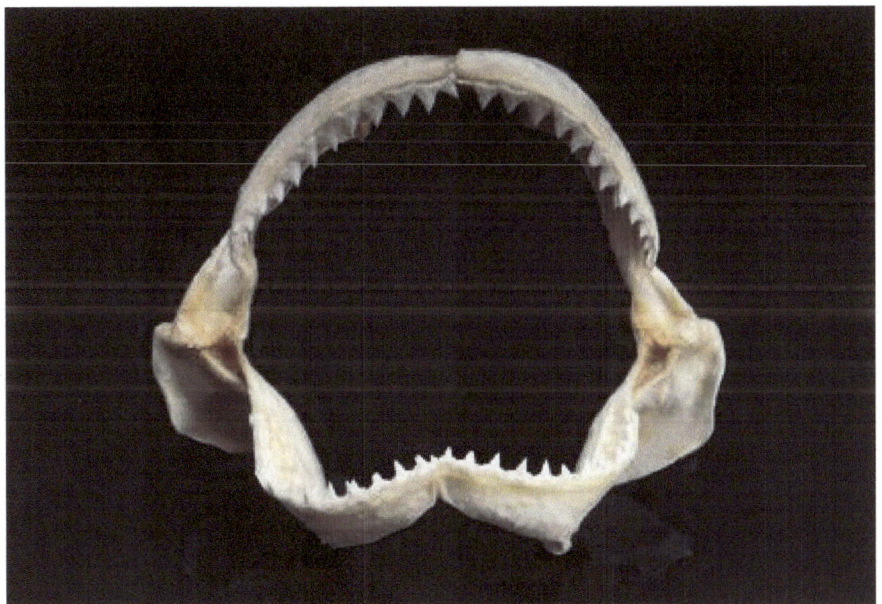

Shark Jaws © josephblake - Fotolia.com

But that's not all there is to a shark is there? Of course it's not, sharks have many interesting parts of their bodies you wouldn't expect, some of which are similar to our bodies and some that are totally different. You may think there's no way sharks can be similar, they swim under water.

You're right, sharks do swim underwater but they need oxygen like we do to breath. But how can they breath under water if we can't breathe under water? Well sharks have what are called gills instead of lungs. Gills allow sharks to use dissolved oxygen in the water they swim in this allows them to stay underwater without having to come up for air like a human or a whale. Sharks also have a heart just like we do, their hearts pump blood to the rest of their body to keep them going the same as ours.

If you've ever tried opening your jaw really wide you may have noticed that only the bottom part of your jaw opens and the top part stays where it is. This is exactly the same as a sharks mouth and jaw. When a shark eats smaller fish, the food is stored inside a stomach. Their stomachs work the same way ours do by using stomach acids to digest the food and turn it into energy. The big fin at the back of their body is called the Caudal Fin. This is the part of their body that propels the shark forward in the water and steers them in a certain direction.

Sharks have a lot in common with us, they need oxygen and blood to survive, and food to live. They may seem very different but we can't forget the similarities.

10. Misunderstandings about Sharks

Misunderstandings about sharks are many, you may have heard of sharks displayed in movies and storybooks to be possessing different characteristics that are unpleasant. They sometimes portray sharks as the predators for man or creatures which hunts man for food in case a man lands in the sea where they are present. The following are common misunderstandings about sharks.

1. Shark always hunt man for food.

This is a misunderstanding. The truth is that most sharks will tend to eat many things that come their way while in water. In case a man comes their way they can eat him, not necessarily hunting for man while swimming in beaches as movies and story books depict.

2. Sharks never rests they are in constant motion

This is a misunderstanding of the sharks as there are studies showing that sharks do rest. For example recent studies show that there are sharks that rest in caves in Japan and Mexico. The idea that sharks will draw and suffocate if they rest on water is just a misconception.

3. Misunderstanding that sharks do not have minds

Sharks have been discovered to have well-functioning body system with brains. Sharks can have senses such as smell, hearing ,sight, and electro senses .Experiments have been carried out concerning this and scientist have proved for sharks to be responding and even getting to learn when trained.

4. Sharks are color blind

This is a misunderstanding in many people that has been proved wrong by scientist after testing sharks with different colors and the sharks were able to respond differently indicating they have a sense of color.

5. Sharks do not hear

This is a misunderstanding that has been proved by scientist to be wrong. Studies have indicated that sharks can hear over a long distance more than man and can hear considerably low sounds as compared.

6. Sharks are useless animals

This is a misconception that has been put wrong where scientist have carried out useful experiments using sharks. Some fishermen even catch sharks to skin for their useful hides.

Read More Amazing Animal Books

Purchase at Amazon.com

Download Free Books!
http://MendonCottageBooks.com

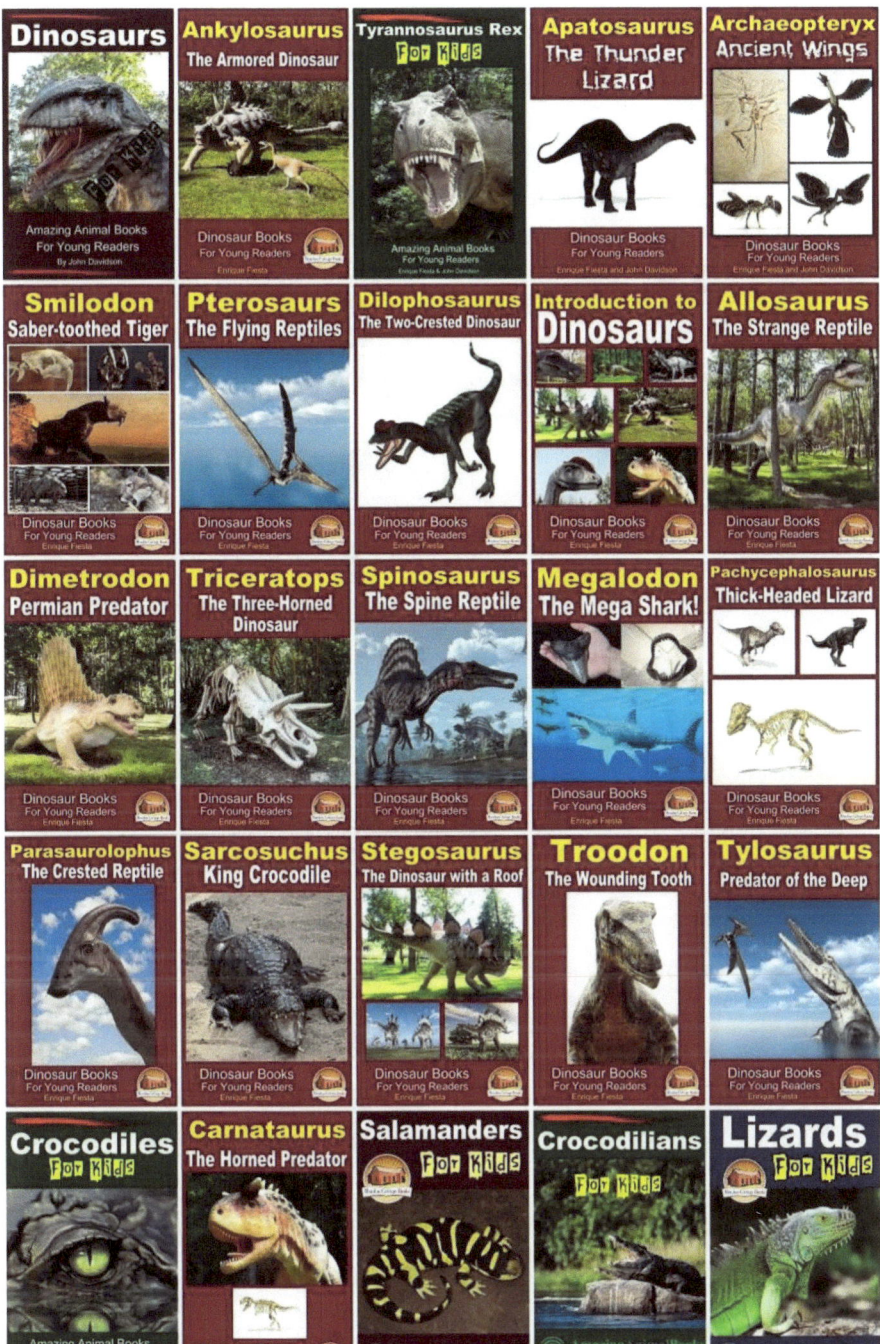

Our books are available at

1. Amazon.com
2. Barnes and Noble
3. Itunes
4. Kobo
5. Smashwords
6. Google Play Books

Download Free Books!
http://MendonCottageBooks.com

Publisher

JD-Biz Corp

P O Box 374

Mendon, Utah 84325

http://www.jd-biz.com/

www.ingramcontent.com/pod-product-compliance
Lightning Source LLC
Chambersburg PA
CBHW050849290526
45792CB00002B/577

* 9 7 8 1 5 1 7 3 6 4 7 3 1 *